THE CHP BO

GREAT ESCAPES

Editor: **Norman Shrive**

Art Director: **Chris Walker**

Contributors: Janet Stewart, Nancy Hamilton, Monique Hammel, Bob Goodwin, Peter Robertson, Christine Racki, Teri Kelly, Diane Campbell, George Stewart

Illustrators: Chris Walker, Gord Frazer, Gary Wein, John DeCosta, Tim Zeltner, Larry MacDougall, Eugene Pawczuk

3312 Mainway, Burlington, Ontario L7M 1A7, Canada
2045 Niagara Falls Blvd., Unit 14, Niagara Falls, NY 14304, U.S.A.

Printed in Hong Kong

Copyright © 1988 by Hayes Publishing Ltd.

All rights reserved. No part of this book may be reproduced or transmitted in any form or by any means, electronic or mechanical, including photocopying, recording or by any information storage and retrieval system, without permission from the publisher.

Contents

Runaway Train 4
A Holiday Nightmare 7
The Third Balloon 8
The Underground Railway 12
Escape Across the Sea 16
General Giraud 20
Escape from Alcatraz 24
Death Sentence 27
A Song for Salvation 30
Wooden Horse 34
Escape from the Tower of London 37
Journey to Freedom 38
Escape of a Sewer Rat 42
Escape to the Past 44

Runaway Train

As the runaway freight train hurtled down the mountainside, all those aboard knew there would be a crash.

It was the early hours of November 22, 1977, as the CPR train traveled through the darkness of Glacier National Park in British Columbia. Seven diesel engines were hauling about one hundred cars loaded with coal to Vancouver. Steep grades and sharp curves make this the most dangerous stretch of track in Canada. To make matters worse, it had been snowing for days.

As the train started down the mountainside it began picking up speed in excess of the recommended ten miles per hour. One of the engineers pushed the button to brake. The brakes weren't holding! He tried again and again, but their speed continued to build.

The conductor and brakeman, who were in the caboose, were very worried as they contacted the engineers. It was obvious to them all: They were on a runaway train and there was nothing they could do.

The train soon was pitching wildly from side to side. Terrified, the crew expected to derail at any moment. Should they take their chances and jump the train? The senior engineer decided to stay to the end.

The two men in the caboose made their decision. They quickly disconnected the caboose from the rest of the train. They were then able to use the caboose's own brakes to bring them to a stop.

The train was now going about eighty-five miles per hour. As it rounded a bad curve and thundered onto a bridge, a steel bar snapped between two of the engines. The cars jackknifed, broke apart and crashed down an embankment to the river below, scattering thousands of tons of coal. As the diesel fuel caught fire, there were several explosions. Damage was immense. More than half of the engines and at least seventy-six coal cars were wrecked. The track and bridge would require extensive repairs.

The three men in the engine were fortunate. Once the train broke loose, they were free of the immense weight pushing them on. It was then possible for them to brake their engine and what was left of the train.

Everyone had made the right decision at the right time. Despite the enormous disaster, there were no injuries.

Holiday Nightmare

African tulip trees, hibiscus and poinsettias grow in bright colors all over the island of Puerto Rico. Surrounded by the blue-green waters of the Atlantic Ocean and the Caribbean Sea, Puerto Rico is a favorite spot for North American tourists.

Nineteen-year-old Mark Silverberg and his two younger sisters, Marla and Marci, were excited about spending their Christmas holidays at the beautiful twenty-one-story, 450-room hotel in San Juan, the capital.

On December 31, 1986, the three young people were relaxing by the pool. Suddenly, the calm was shattered by a terrible explosion. People were screaming and running from the hotel. Smoke was pouring into the sky.

Trapped by a high concrete wall with barbed wire on one side and the fire-engulfed hotel on the other, Mark and his two sisters tried not to panic and looked for a way to escape.

With crowds of people running away from the fire pressing against them, Mark and his sisters ran to the wall. Helping each other, they climbed up the wall and over the dangerously sharp wire. They were soon safe on the beach, breathing great sighs of relief. Looking back at the hotel, they realized how lucky they were to have escaped such a terrible fire.

The Third Balloon

Peter Strelzyk was shaking with cold and fear. He gripped the iron post at one corner of the makeshift gondola and looked out into the night.

He and some friends had taken off ten minutes before and were now floating at about two thousand meters above the ground. A strong wind was pushing them toward West Germany. Their dream was coming true — they were escaping the Communist society they had been forced to live in since birth.

He glanced over his shoulder at the others. His wife Doris was crouched on a platform near the four bottles of propane gas they were using for fuel. Petra Wetzel and the four children huddled together. They were all shivering. This high in the air it was very cold. Gunter Wetzel was standing at the far corner, looking out, and as Peter watched him, his friend turned and gave him a small, hopeful smile.

Peter looked up at the mouth of the balloon where the flame from the burner entered, heating the air inside and causing the balloon to float. The material around the balloon's opening was burned, reminding Peter that the flight was almost over before it began. As they were about to take off, the balloon caught fire, and it was only Gunter's quick action with the fire extinguisher that had saved them. The flame was burning safely now, however, and they were floating steadily. Still, Peter thought, it was not a good beginning.

There had been many problems to overcome. Posneck, the small East German town they lived in, was only sixty kilometers from the border of West Germany, but it may as well have been a million. The border was guarded by soldiers with machine guns and vicious dogs, and the area around it planted with land mines and barbed wire.

Peter, Doris, Gunter and Petra dreamed of living in a country of their choice. They wanted their children to grow up in freedom, where they could read, talk and travel as they pleased.

Early in 1978, Peter and Gunter came up with the idea of flying over the border in a balloon. Trying to leave a Communist country is a very serious crime. If anyone had found out what they were planning, they would have been arrested. They had to do it secretly. And now, on September 15, 1979, they were actually on their way.

As he stood thinking, Peter heard a tearing sound above him and felt a gust of wind on his head. The gondola went dark. "The burner's gone out!" Gunter cried. "There's a rip in the top of the balloon!"

Peter saw the sparks as Gunter tried desperately to relight the burner. "The flame must have been too big," Peter said. "It built up too much pressure inside the balloon." The light flared and the flame was back; they would have to watch it carefully.

This was the third balloon they had built and the only one that had worked. Peter was a mechanic and an electrician. Gunter had worked as a repairman and electrician. Both had technical education and experience, but neither had ever tried to build a balloon.

Long months of hard work and worry had led up to this: driving to a larger town to find material; Gunter sewing secretly for weeks, while Peter constructed the heating system and gondola to carry them; and the disappointment when they discovered that the balloon would not hold the air.

They then made a second balloon, driving farther for different material so no one would get suspicious. This time the burner didn't produce enough heat to lift them. Then, one day, Peter discovered a way to make it work. Their hopes high, the family and friends took off. But they ran into a cloud and came down right near the border, still in East Germany. They had to leave the balloon, and it was found the next day by border guards. Now it was a race against time for they knew that sooner or later they would be caught.

All of a sudden a light beamed up at them from the darkness below. Peter gasped. "Searchlights!" He reached quickly for the burner and turned the flame up to its full height. They sat, silent and scared, waiting. The balloon continued to float.

Peter suddenly heard someone behind him cry out. He turned just in time to see the flame flicker and go out. Gunter knelt beside the burner, trying desperately to bring it back. "We're out of gas," he said softly. "That hole," he muttered. "It made us use up the gas too fast." They looked at the scared faces of their wives and children. The balloon began to fall.

Suddenly, the platform struck something, jarring them off their feet. They bounced, then hit the hard ground. The gondola was still.

They stood up and began to walk, looking around cautiously. When they reached some trees, Gunter turned and said, "Women and children wait here. Peter and I will look around."

The moon shone brightly as the two men carefully made their way. Soon they came to a barn. They entered it quietly and gasped as they saw what was written on the side of a wagon: The name of the farmer who owned it! In the East, this was never done.

Suddenly, they heard a car pull up and looked at each other. It was now or never. They went outside. Two policemen were coming toward them. "Did we make it?" shouted Peter. "Are we in the West?" called Gunter.

The two officers smiled at them. "Yes," they said. "Congratulations!"

Peter and Gunter hugged each other, laughing with joy. They had done it! They had flown to freedom!

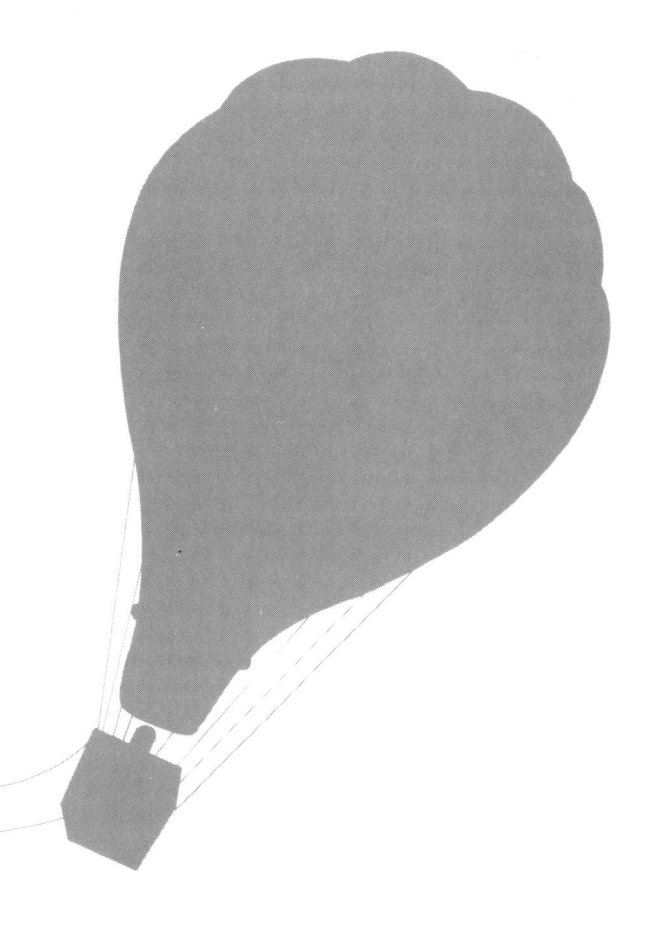

J.F. DECOSTA · 1987 ·

The Underground Railway

"Keep running," Jeb Moses told his wife and small son. "Head for the river and don't look back."

Far in the distance, away from the beech woods, the sound of barking dogs could be heard, followed by the shouts and curses of angry men.

"Keep going," he whispered. "We've got to reach the river before they catch us."

"I'm so tired," said his wife Molly. "My legs hurt."

Jeb paused and leaned against a tree. He shivered in the unusually cold night. He looked up and smiled. On that September night in Louisiana, he could see, clear and bright, the North Star.

"Our guide," he said, pointing straight up at the star, "that will surely lead us out of slavery."

"Will that star take us all the way to Canada?" Henry asked his father.

"It will, son. It surely will." Jeb Moses, his wife Molly, and seven-year-old son Henry, were runaway black slaves from a Louisiana cotton plantation.

*"Let's get moving,"
Jeb said. "Those slave
catchers are right on our heels."
If they were caught, Jeb knew
they would be returned to his master,
punished, and perhaps
separated forever.*

After another half hour of stumbling and falling through the heavy underbrush, Jeb paused and listened. He could still hear the dogs getting closer, but now there was a new sound. Water! Rushing water! The river.

"Come on," he shouted, no longer afraid of being heard by their pursurers. "We're near the river."

They ran out of the woods and stood on the bank of a swift-flowing river.

"It has to be here somewhere," Jeb cried, frantically tearing through the underbrush covering the riverbank. "Mr. Hawkins told me it would be here."

"Here it is, Daddy," Henry shouted excitedly. "I've found the boat."

Jeb rushed to his son's side, pulling away the covering of brambles and sumach leaves, revealing a small rowboat. Jeb helped his son and wife inside the boat before pushing it into the swiftly flowing Mississippi river. They were on the first leg of a long and dangerous voyage to freedom and a new life in Canada.

*As they disappeared
into the darkness,
a forty-year-old white
man watched them
from the other side of the river.*

He was Mr. Hawkins, a dealer in lumber from Ohio who often visited the southern United States, including Louisiana. He often talked with poor black slaves like Jeb who worked on the huge cotton and rice plantations. He learned about the terrible lives Jeb and his family led.

At first, slaves had been black men and women who were kidnapped from their homes on the west coast of Africa and who were brought by force to America and sold to plantation owners. The slaves were made to grow rice, tobacco or cotton and in return were given coarse food, housed in tiny shacks, and forbidden to leave the plantation without permission.

Later on, when it became illegal to bring in slaves from Africa, the law stated that the children of black slaves were also slaves. Jeb and his family were born slaves. Jeb told Mr. Hawkins about how he and Molly were whipped if they complained or disobeyed orders and about how Henry wasn't allowed to go to school. Slaves were not allowed to learn how to read or write.

14

*It wasn't a
real railroad,
but a secret route
of escape.*

Mr. Hawkins, like many people from the north, was opposed to slavery. He was called an "abolitionist," meaning he wanted an end to slavery. He also decided to help Jeb escape to the north through the Underground Railroad. It wasn't a real railroad, but a secret route of escape. Mr. Hawkins had left Jeb the rowboat, but he had also explained how to find "stations" or safe places to hide from slave hunters. The stations were run by "conductors," men like Mr. Hawkins, who risked imprisonment, fines and even death to house, feed, clothe and direct the Moses family on their way northward.

Molly was often afraid, not only that they might be caught and forced back to Louisiana, but also of what they might find in Canada. Her master had said that Canada was very cold and that all Canadians spoke French. He also said that Canadians worshipped idols and executed black men upon arrival.

*"It'll be alright,"
Jeb assured her,
"and we'll be free."*

Reaching Canada was a difficult task. Many runaways died en route or were captured and returned to their owners. Jeb's family travelled by boat and buggy through the slave states to the free northern states where many people helped them.

However, Jeb and his family were not yet safe. Even in cities like Detroit and New York, where many fugitive slaves settled and found work, not everybody was friendly. Some people felt that the ex-slaves threatened to take over their neighborhoods and jobs. Sometimes Jeb's family were treated hostilely, even violently. Once they were warned that a white man who seemed friendly had contacted the slave hunters. He was going to turn the Moses family over to them for a reward!

Jeb decided his family would be safer in the British colony of Canada. In 1833, the British abolished slavery in all her colonies. Unlike in the United States, Canadian law did not consider a runaway slave a criminal and in Canada there was less chance of Jeb's family being forced to return to Louisiana.

In Detroit, Jeb and his family took a steamer called the Arrow across the Great Lakes to a small port in Canada West as Ontario was then called. Jeb was able to get a small farm through working on the railroad.

Jeb, Molly and Henry stayed in Canada, even though President Abraham Lincoln eventually freed all the slaves in the United States. The Moses family was part of several thousand fugitive slaves who successfully traveled the whole length of the Underground Railway, from Louisiana to Canada, following the North Star as their guide.

Escape Across The Sea

Major Geoffrey Rowley was one of the youngest divisional commanders of the British infantry. At the age of 29, he was responsible for the operation of an anti-aircraft defense unit. The Major didn't have a great deal of experience in actual combat, but this would soon change.

17

On February 8, 1942, three Japanese army divisions, consisting of twenty-three thousand soldiers, made their way in a night attack over the straits using two hundred collapsible boats and one hundred larger landing craft. They were masters of seaborne landing and skilled in jungle warfare.

Meanwhile, Japanese bombers quickly filled the skies, appearing like a swarm of locusts. Then suddenly, the burst of anti-aircraft fire cracked the silent air. One by one the bombs dropped from the intruding aircraft, hitting the ground with ear-splitting explosions. The earth shook beneath Major Rowley's feet. He was perspiring; his eyes, mouth and ears filled with dust and sand.

At last the raid ended. Major Rowley and his men cautiously got up from where they were lying and peered over the rim of their tattered trenches. The dust was still settling as Major Rowley began assessing the damage and casualties.

Later that day a message from headquarters in Britain came through the wire. Captain Kennard received the information first. Headquarters instructed the battalion to surrender. They went on to say those trying to flee Singapore were unsuccessful. Out of fifty ships that sailed from the island packed with evacuees destined for India (one of Britain's allies), forty had been sunk.

After hearing the news from headquarters, Major Rowley and Captain Kennard met privately to discuss their next move. Rowley told Kennard of a Chinese boat anchored at a nearby harbor and also told him of his planned escape across the open sea. Although it was risky, Kennard agreed they had to try. Rowley then informed the men of his intention.

He explained to the men that this plan of escape from the island would be extremely dangerous. Not only would they be sitting ducks for the Japanese, they could also be mistaken for the enemy by the British Navy. This was a distinct possibility, considering that they were planning to escape in a Chinese boat named Joan. The Major waited for their reaction to his plan. He thought only a small number of the men would choose to join him and Captain Kennard. However, after a moment of silence, the entire platoon voiced their approval. Rowley knew the greater the number, the greater the risk, but the Major was not going to leave any of his men behind.

Early the next morning, they began their journey aboard the Joan, an Asian boat known as a Chinese junk. The men had to use oars to power the vessel. The idea was to use the Chinese junk to cross the Maracca Strait to Padung.

They weren't at sea for very long when the first sign of trouble appeared. Rowing toward the Joan was a group of Malay warriors.

Malays, the native people of the islands, were victims of the war. They were not formally on one side or the other. However, they were warriors, and their reaction to the intruding vessel was unpredictable. The men held their breath as the approaching boat drew near. One of the British soldiers bent down to pick up his rifle. Rowley quickly grabbed the gun and put it down by his feet.

Fortunately, Fraser, one of the British soldiers on board, spoke Malayanese. Under orders from Major Rowley, Fraser addressed the leader of the Malay warriors. They spoke for some time as the rest of the men waited anxiously. All of a sudden the chief made a motion familiar to Malay custom meaning "good-bye and good luck."

Major Rowley and his men reached Padang on the afternoon of March 10, 1942. Rowley went directly to Colonel Warren's office, the Royal Marine Commander stationed in Pedang. Warren told Rowley that a small ship, the Sederhana Djohanis, was sailing for India the next day. This was the break they needed. It gave the British soldiers the best chance of escaping alive.

Rowley awoke the next morning to discover that the boat was already moving through the rocky inlets of the island. He shook Fraser and whispered excitedly, "We're off."

As the men were assigned their duties, the Djohanis moved across the sparkling sea. The pleasantness of the trip came to an abrupt end as white edges showed on the rims of the waves. The ship's mast creaked as sails tightened and strained against the wind. The ship pitched and swayed, causing the men's few personal possessions to scatter across the boat. After hours of rainfall and heavy winds, the storm finally ended.

The men's attention now turned to the possibilities of enemy aircraft. Their safety depended on the Japanese pilots believing that the Djohanis was a fishing vessel.

The British soldiers had been at sea for more than two weeks and had passed the halfway point of their journey. Even though it was common to see the occasional Japanese aircraft streak by in the distance, the men were very afraid they would be caught.

On the morning of March 29, a plane circled overhead and began to descend. The Major yelled for cover as the men dispersed in all directions. The small bomber unloaded an arsenal of machine-gun fire on the Djohanis. The men listened in silence as the engines of the plane faded away.

They were lucky to have escaped the deadly bullets. But survival was still very difficult.

Their water supply was running critically low, and they were very restless. It had been ten days since the attack and four weeks since their departure. The men were becoming desperate for some kind of sign that their journey would soon end.

The next day that sign appeared as a flock of birds flew overhead, indicating they were close to land. The anticipation grew as the men searched for land as far as they could see. Their spirits dipped once more as the search for land remained unanswered. It was possible that the birds had originated from a small island that may have been small enough that they could have passed it unnoticed during the night.

Later that afternoon a ship was spotted. The men prayed that it was one of their own. As the ship got closer, it was clear that it belonged to the British Navy. The Major and the rest of the men were lifted aboard the Anglo-Canadian. The journey to India had ended, and it became apparent that they had made a remarkable escape after the invasion of Singapore.

20

GENERAL GIRAUD

In World War I, Captain Henri Giraud was wounded in a bayonet charge at Charleroi. His comrades left him for dead. The Germans took him to a Belgian prison camp, but took no special precautions as they believed him to be too ill to escape.

But, before his wounds had healed, he escaped from the prison camp by pretending to be a Belgian circus performer. When he got to Brussels, a nurse named Edith Cavell, who often assisted Allied officers, helped Giraud escape to Holland.

Eventually, Giraud was able to rejoin his regiment in France. Between the wars he served in Africa. When the Second World War came, he was appointed commander-in-chief of the Allied Forces in Laon.

Giraud faced the full thrust of the German breakthrough in the Ardennes. Although sixty-one years old, he still went to the front to see whether the German advance could be checked. It was there that the Germans captured him. They hoped to use him to learn military secrets.

Giraud was taken to the German fortress of Konigstein, a prison situated on a very high cliff. The Germans were determined that Giraud would not escape.

But nothing could stop Giraud from planning his getaway. First he improved his knowledge of German. Giraud knew that unless he could speak German, he would never be able to escape from Konigstein. He could speak it a little, but he practiced daily until he was without a suspicion of a French accent. Giraud also managed to copy a map of the neighboring countryside. He spent hours and hours memorizing it, and finally burned it.

Fortunately there were people inside France anxious to assist Giraud's escape. Without their help he might never have gotten away from Konigstein.

Friends sent him packages tied with twine which he used to make a rope. When he had completed the rope, Giraud knew it wouldn't be strong enough to support him. So he wrote letters in code to his wife asking for copper wire to strengthen the rope.

His wife passed the coded letters on to his main helpers who sent him a ham. When Giraud cut the ham he found copper wire hidden inside.

All this scheming took the best part of two years. Giraud now had the means to escape, but had a problem trying to disguise his blue uniform, commonly worn by French Generals. His raincoat would pass for civilian clothing, but what he badly needed was an ordinary hat. Some time passed and Giraud received another ham. Inside was an ordinary hat.

On April 17, 1942, Giraud went on to the balcony overlooking the sentry walk. He had fixed a package to his waist containing his raincoat, the hat, some chocolates and biscuits.

When the guard was farthest from him, Giraud swiftly knotted the top of the rope to the balcony and began his long descent down the cliff. He had gloves, but even so the descent was painful and cut his skin.

Giraud's attempt to escape went against all physical odds. He was over sixty, and his old wounds from the bayonet charge still pained him. By the time he reached the ground, he could only limp slowly away from the jail. He finally reached a small wood where he shaved off his moustache, put on his hat and raincoat, and limped for almost an hour to a bridge.

In his tired and injured state, Giraud couldn't have accomplished much more. But the coded messages he sent to his wife had worked well. Giraud was met at the bridge by a man who took him to a nearby station where he gave Giraud a suitcase containing clothes, forged identity papers and money.

*On the train, Giraud changed into his new clothes.
Then what he dreaded happened.*

A full description of Giraud was wired around Germany within hours. The description mentioned that Giraud was over six feet tall, something he couldn't disguise. But the general hadn't wasted his two years of planning; he had realized long ago that the search would be as thorough as the Germans could make it. His tactic was to change trains frequently, edging toward the French border, but never staying too long in one train.

On three occasions Giraud was actually leaving a train as Gestapo officers were boarding it. On another occasion, when the Gestapo searched his train, Giraud saved himself by talking with a German officer in the Afrika Corps.

The search for Giraud was so intense that he couldn't cross the border into France. German guards were posted at all frontier posts on the railway, and they had strict instructions to stop all men six feet tall. So the general headed for Switzerland. Finally, through Switzerland, he made his escape. The Germans insisted that the Swiss should send him back. The Swiss, arguing that they were neutral, refused. On the other hand, the Swiss would not let him go to France.

The Gestapo still hunted for Giraud in Switzerland; their agents closed in on his hiding place.

But he escaped again, changing cars every few minutes. Finally, after days and days of anxiety and distress, Giraud arrived in that part of France which the Germans left unoccupied by their forces. But Giraud was still forced to hide; the Nazis even formed a plot to assassinate him.

But now the British and the Americans needed General Giraud. They were planning the invasion of North Africa and knew that Giraud would make a great leader of a pro-Allied French force in Algeria. A message was sent arranging for Giraud to be smuggled across the Mediterranean sea.

A few nights later a British submarine was sent to France to pick up Giraud and bring him to North Africa where he helped pave the way for an Allied victory. Even in his mid-sixties, Giraud was an invaluable leader in the war. His harrowing escapes let him remain active as he fought for his country.

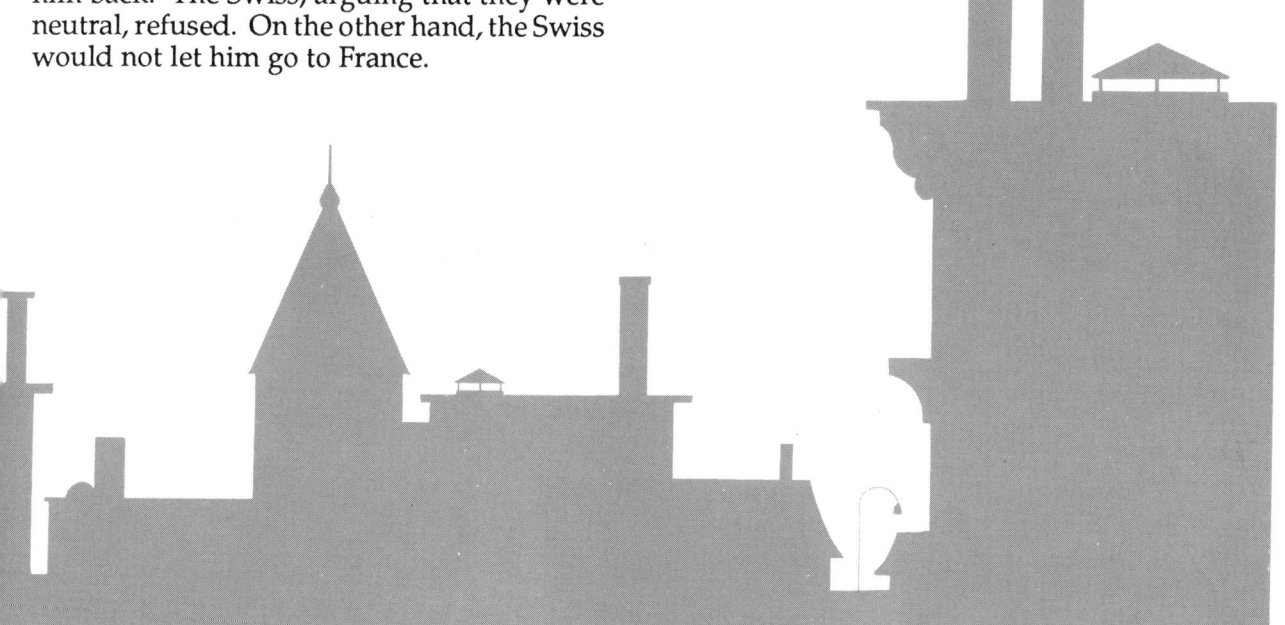

24

Escape from Alcatraz

The three heroes of this story are to be admired for their ingenuity and clever means of escape. But their heroism ends here, for these men were bank robbers and notorious men of violence who were sentenced for ten to fifteen years in the infamous Alcatraz Prison.

Located a short distance off the coast of California, in San Francisco Bay, is the small island called Alcatraz. Also known as "the Rock," it had a reputation of being one of the most repelling and frightening places on earth. Alcatraz, meaning Island of Pelicans, got its name from the Spaniards who found that the pelicans inhabiting the island in the eighteenth century were the only living creatures able to come and go freely.

25

The island was so isolated that in 1934 the U.S. government decided it was a perfect location for a prison. Before this time it was used as a military prison. Glorified mobsters such as Al Capone, George "Machine Gun" Kelly and "Doc" Barker spent time in Alcatraz Prison. The prison boasted that it was inescapable. All news from the outside world was forbidden. Inmates were also forbidden to talk to one another for fear of banishment to the "isolation" cell - a completely dark, freezing cell with no furniture. Throughout the prison, no newspapers or radios were allowed, and inmates could only discuss family news in letters or during family visits.

The hand-picked guards carried machine guns at all times. High brick walls were built around the prison, and the cell doors were double-locked. The strong tidal currents of the surrounding San Francisco Bay made swimming to shore impossible. With these deterrants it was surprising that three prisoners, Frank Lee Morris, John Anglin and his brother Clarence Anglin were planning an escape attempt from this incredible fortress.

The year was 1962. The salt air gusting from the bay had been hitting the outside walls of the prison for some time. Noticing that the plaster crumbled at the slightest force, Frank Morris made his master plan. He and the Anglin brothers stole tablespoons from the dining hall and, removing the metal grills from the air vents in their cell walls, dug chunks from the weakened plaster and cement walls. Night after night, between hourly guard checks, the three convicts carefully dug the vent holes larger and larger. They made cardboard grills to cover the ever-expanding holes so they wouldn't be noticed by the guards during the day. The powdered concrete and plaster they were chipping from the walls was becoming a problem. The men disposed of some of it by flushing the powder down the toilets and stuffing some into their pockets which they then scattered during their outside courtyard exercises.

Then, on June 22, 1962, the three made their escape. They were prepared for the 9:30 p.m. bedcheck. They cleverly made "dummy" heads of themselves from plaster, paint and hair scraps they had gathered from the prison barber shop. They stuffed pillows onto their cots, and from a short distance it appeared as though real men were asleep in their cells.

Although the holes the men had dug in the wall weren't quite big enough, they managed to push through them into a seldom-used utility corridor behind the cell wall. From this corridor they climbed up a long pipe to an air conditioning vent, pried it loose, and squeezed through to the rooftop above. Once on the roof, they were dangerously close to the guard post at the number one tower at the northern end of the prison compound. Fortunately for the prisoners, they were not noticed by the guards. They scurried across the roof, then slid down an outside drainpipe. At last they were on the ground outside the prison compound. They skillfully scaled a high fence topped with barbed wire and scrambled to the northeast corner of the island to the water's edge.

Throughout the night, guards made their rounds through the darkened prison corridors, but saw nothing strange as they passed the empty cells of the three escaped convicts. It was not until early the next morning, when the inmates stood before their cells for a head count, that they found the three convicts had escaped. Within hours, dozens of armed hunters with bloodhounds scoured the island, and boats searched the bay area.

Days later, a fourth prisoner who had also planned to escape with Morris and the Anglin brothers but had backed out at the last minute, told guards that the escaped convicts used inflated prison raincoats to serve as a rubber raft to carry them to nearby Angel Island and then to the mainland.

Frank Morris, John and Clarence Anglin were never heard of again. It is believed that the men successfully escaped from Alcatraz.

In 1963, after thirty years standing as an incredible fortress, Alcatraz closed its crumbling doors forever.

DEATH SENTENCE

He was trapped. Thomas Tribbles knew there could be no escape from the two men who were blocking the doorway of his hotel room.

They stood, pointing their guns squarely at him. Thomas was lying on the bed, weary and aching from his recent journey. One move to get to the window or to try to push past them into the corridor and that would be that: the two men would shoot him down without a moment's thought.

They were border ruffians: lawless...without conscience or mercy. Their leader, William Titus, was one of the most feared and hated criminals in the whole of the central United States. Titus would kidnap Negro slaves from plantations and sell them to new masters. He was especially hated by the abolitionists, the people who wanted to end slavery.

Thomas Tribbles, although only eighteen years old, fought against slavery. The two ruffians ordered young Thomas to his feet. Then one of them grabbed him by the shoulder and pushed him through the door of the room. They were going to the ruffians' camp outside town.

The people in the street knew what was happening, and they ran and hid.

Thomas didn't blame them. They were afraid and wanted to avoid trouble. They knew that if the border ruffians got upset, they were quite capable of shooting up a whole town or setting it on fire. No one on that hot afternoon in 1856 possessed the courage that made Thomas Tribbles risk his life for a cause. Thomas had become well-known as a fearless, outspoken campaigner against slavery, traveling from one small town to another. He raged against plantation owners who worked their slaves until they dropped in the fields or beat them or otherwise ill-treated them. Tribbles preached that slavery was an act of inhumanity and wickedness and had to be abolished.

At the age of eleven, Thomas had been taken from his mother and father and forced to work for a cotton farmer in Iowa. The man had forced Thomas to work in the fields from four in the morning until nearly midnight. Then, after a light meal, Thomas was allowed only a few hours' sleep on rough straw in the barn before he was driven back to the fields to labor through another eighteen-hour day. After a year he ran away.

He toured the mid-West during the summer of 1856, speaking out against slavery and slave owners, especially Colonel William Titus. Titus decided that Thomas was one abolitionist who must be silenced, so he sent two of his ruffians to kidnap him.

Titus was ready and waiting for Thomas as soon as the two ruffians marched him into camp.

There was to be a trial the next morning, and the charge was "being an abolitionist" and preaching abolitionism in public. Thomas knew what the verdict would be and he wondered why Titus would bother with a trial.

The trial began the next morning. Thomas took the opportunity to speak out against slavery. He noted with despair that the jury, especially selected by Titus, included men like the local sheriff and the United States marshal. The jury arrived at the "guilty" verdict: a sentence of death by hanging.

After the trial, Thomas was marched back to the border ruffians' camp, thrown into a shed and made to lie face down on the ground. He overheard an officer say that there were armed abolitionists in the area.

*Thomas fell asleep.
Shooting nearby woke him at dawn.
A shadow fell over him.
A guard was ready to fire.*

Thomas sprang up, threw himself at the gun and jerked the barrel out of the way. A bullet ripped through Thomas' shirt. Another bullet hit the guard. Thomas grabbed the gun and escaped outside.

In the streets abolitionists were fighting the ruffians. Thomas crouched down and ran across the camp with cross-fire flying around him. He reached the officers' quarters and found Colonel Titus propped up against the wall. Titus was badly bleeding and in a lot of pain.

Thomas stood there. As soon as Titus saw Thomas he began to cry for mercy. His hand trembled violently as he put it up to defend himself if Thomas shot. He would do anything, he told Thomas, so long as Thomas would let him live.

Thomas saw a pitiful Titus - a coward. But Thomas showed mercy, and shortly after, Titus and the ruffians surrendered.

In 1861, the ruffians and abolitionists faced each other during the American Civil War, a war that divided the American southern states, who wanted slavery, and the northern states, who wanted to abolish it.

*In 1865, the North won,
and slavery was abolished.*

After the war, Thomas Tribbles turned his cause toward championing another oppressed people - the American Indians.

The few hours, however, that Thomas had spent under the sentence of death in the ruffian camp remained a vivid memory for the rest of his life. It was, Thomas wrote, the "most nerve-wracking escape of my life." When Titus surrendered to the abolitionists who invaded his camp, it was 7:00 in the morning. Only one hour later and Thomas would have ended his life on the gallows.

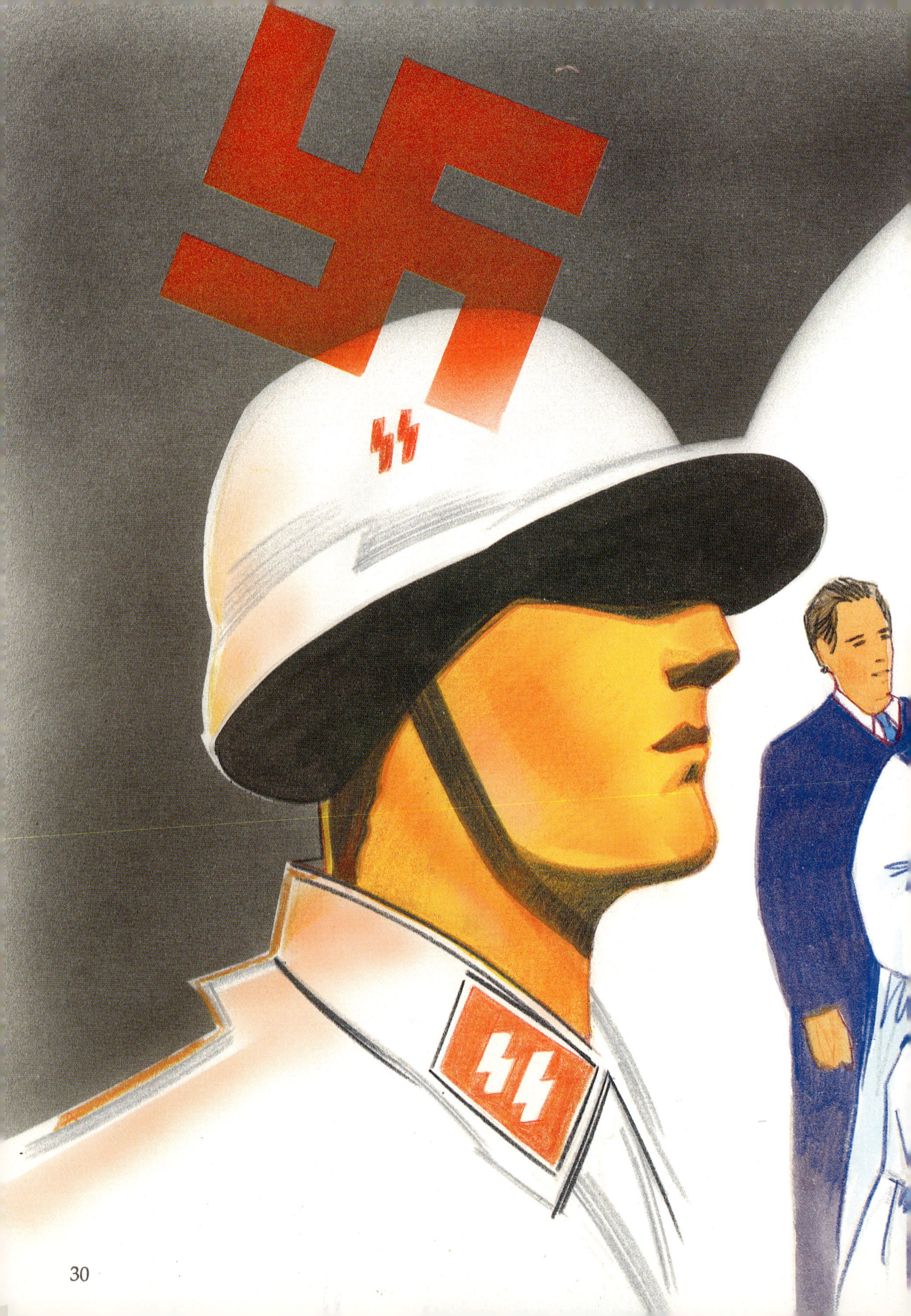

A Song for Salvation

The Trapp family loved to sing. It was their one great pastime and pleasure. Little did they know that their singing would eventually lead to their salvation.

The Trapp family, consisting of Mama Maria Augusta, Papa Georg, and seven daughters and three sons, once lived in a large, graceful mansion in Salzburg, Austria. Maria would take her family to the back garden where they would sing in joyous harmony while Maria accompanied them on her guitar. A neighbor, passing by one day, heard the delightful voices of the young children and entered them in a singing festival contest. They won first prize!

*Disaster soon struck
the noble Trapp family. The bank where
Georg Trapp invested all his savings went
bankrupt.*

It was 1935, and Hitler's Nazis were quietly moving in to Austria. Hitler suspended all tourist trade in Austria, which caused serious problems in the financial world. Georg was devastated. How would he support his family? Maria was not alarmed. Instead, she thought of ways she could earn money. They agreed to turn one of the large downstairs rooms into a chapel, taking in a pastor as a boarder. Within a year they had taken in many young professors and students of the theological faculty, which helped to make ends meet.

Through the publicity of their first singing contest and the necessity for money, the Trapp family turned their singing from a pleasant hobby to a necessary profession. They began touring all of Europe, and soon they were offered a contract to sing in America.

By March, 1938, the Germans had completely invaded Austria. All Austrian citizens who were not loyal members of the Nazi Party were at their mercy. Georg, who was an officer in the Imperial Austrian Navy, was invited by the Nazi's Navy Department to take command of a huge submarine in preparation for the war. Georg, whose love for his native homeland was strong, would not consent to this request.

Another letter from the Nazis was sent to the Trapp family. This time it was addressed to their son, Rupert, who was studying medicine in Innsbruk. The letter requested Rupert to serve as a doctor for the Nazis. Rupert also declined their invitation.

A week later, a call from Munich was received by the Trapp family asking them to sing at Adolf Hitler's birthday party, and once again the Trapps declined the invitation. That made three refusals. The Trapps knew they were in trouble. Refusing three invitations from the Nazis meant the Trapps were not honoring the Nazi Party, and the longer they stayed in Austria, the more dangerous the situation would become for them. They knew they had to leave their beloved home if they wanted to survive and that they would have to leave soon. If the Nazis found them now, they would all be sent to German concentration camps as traitors to the Nazi Party.

*The only place the Trapps
could escape to in order to be
completely safe from Hitler
and the impending war,
was America.*

But how could they get to America without arousing suspicions in the ever-watchful eyes of the Nazis? Quickly and secretly they packed whatever belongings they could carry and left for South Tyrol, Italy, for what appeared to be a mountain-climbing expedition. The very next day the Trapps learned the Nazis had closed the border to Austria, and no one was allowed to exit or enter the country. The Trapps were thankful for their speedy escape, but they were still in grave danger.

They tried to appear as normal and casual as possible on their visit to Italy. Their biggest problem now was money. They wrote to the agent in America who had earlier offered them a contract to sing there. Then they waited. Every day seemed like an eternity. The Nazis were everywhere, always asking questions. The Trapp family carried on as usual, singing in concerts in Italy and mountain climbing in St. Georgen. At this point the Nazis suspected nothing unusual about their behavior.

After three long and frightening weeks, the letter from America arrived. Georg and Maria held their breath. The letter they held in their hands was the deciding factor whether they would survive or not. Maria quickly tore open the envelope and out tumbled enough tickets for the entire family to sail to America. They wept for joy. Late that evening, they boarded a ship that would sail from Italy to London, England. Anxiously waiting for the ship to begin its journey, they were terribly afraid of what would happen if they were caught on board. Then the ship began to move. They breathed sighs of relief.

It was September, 1938. The war in Europe was imminent, and the Trapp family was safe on board an ocean liner to America.

They had sacrificed everything - their lovely home and beloved country - for freedom. The Trapps settled in Vermont and sang all over America and Canada to the delight of thousands of listeners. But they never forgot the terror they had experienced escaping the Nazis.

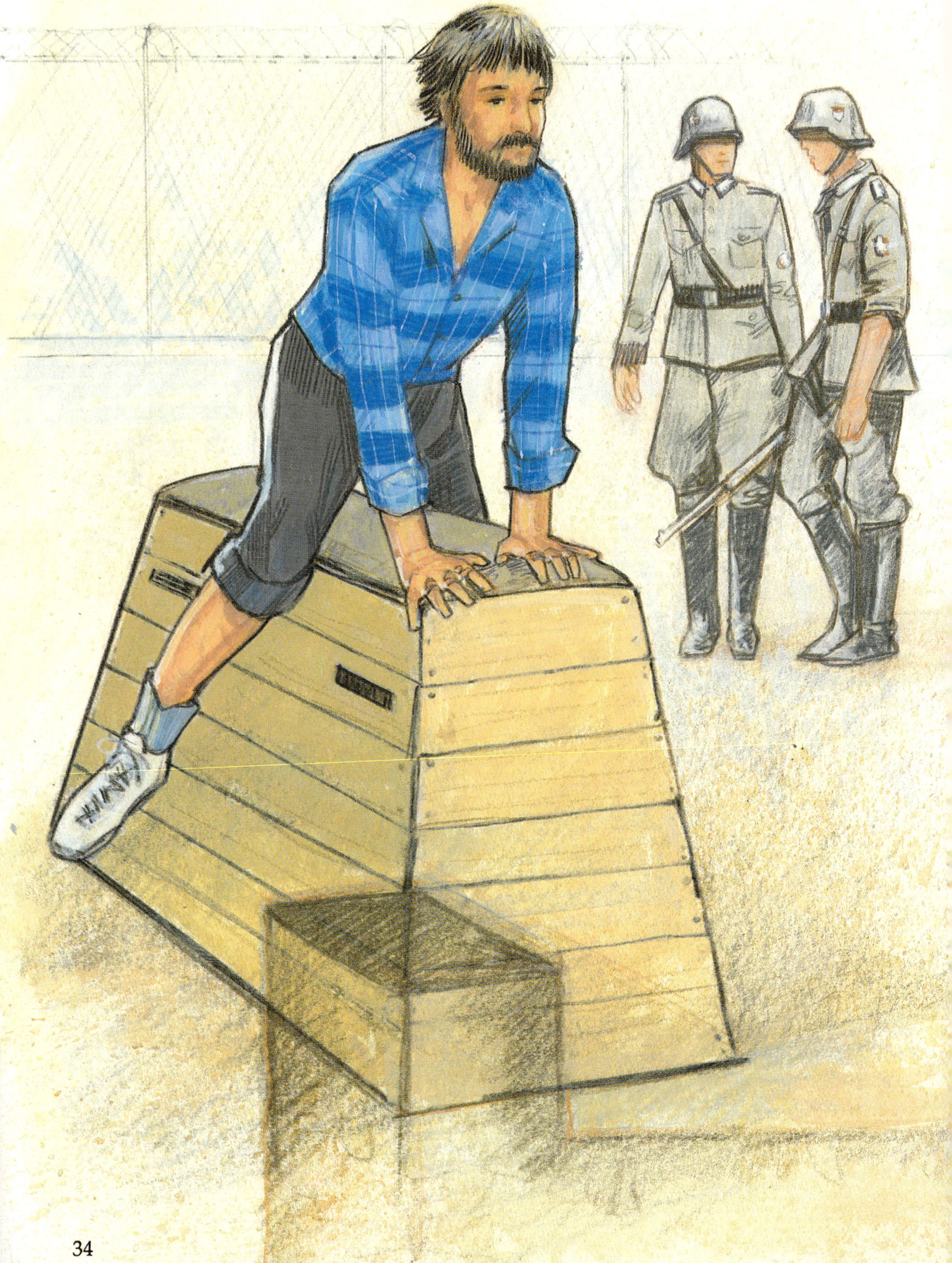

Wooden Horse

The word "vault" has two meanings. As a verb, or action word, to vault means to jump over some thing. As a noun, or naming word, a vault is an underground cavern or tunnel. During World War II, the word "vault" took on both meanings when a courageous trio of British airmen escaped from a heavily guarded Nazi prisoner of war camp in Germany.

It was 1943 and the Germans had won many battles since the war had begun in 1939. But Britain and her allies were determined to resist the powerful German forces until, with growing power and resources, they would eventually defeat the Nazis. Part of this determination was shown in the attempts of Allied flyers to escape from German prisoner-of-war camps so that they could return to England and fly again against the enemy. Many of these men, pilots, navigators, air gunners, were imprisoned in Stalag Luft III near Dresden, Germany. The camp was surrounded by two rows of sharp barbed wire fences with high wooden sentry towers inside the double rows. German soldiers stood guard inside these towers with machine guns and searchlights, watching to see that no one escaped. The Allied soldiers lived in wooden huts in the center of the prison. They were not allowed out of their huts at night. Fierce attack dogs prowled the compound every night, preventing escape.

*Some men had tried to
get away from Stalag Luft III. They
had pried loose floor
boards from underneath
their huts and had built tunnels, but
they were always caught.*

Special machines called seismographs recorded the sounds of digging in the prison. Also, it was just too far from the huts to the barbed wire fence. A better way had to be found. Eric Williams, a British airman, found the way!

Eric, with the help of his friends, Captain Michael Codner and Flight Lieutenant Oliver Philpot, built a vaulting horse from Red Cross plywood food cartons that had been sent from England. The horse measured four feet, six inches high and covered a base area of five feet by three feet. It was hollow inside. Eric convinced the Germans that the English soldiers wanted to use the vaulting horse for gymnastic exercise. The Germans agreed.

Each day, the horse was carried out to a spot about ninety feet from the barbed wire fence. A group of British soldiers practiced vaulting over the horse every day. They did this for two hours at a time. The German guards laughed at the antics of the British prisoners. But the guards didn't know that a British soldier sat inside the horse each day that it was carried out. After the horse was put in position, he would begin tunneling underground toward the barbed wire fence as the man above leaped over the horse. The constant thudding of the vaulter's feet camouflaged the sound of digging, throwing off the sensitive seismograph readings. The dirt that was tunneled out each day was placed in bags that the prisoners had made. At the end of his digging, the soldier would hang the bags of earth on little hooks inside the horse. He would place a small wooden trap door over the hole and cover it with earth. The guards never suspected a thing.

*It took four and a half months
of hard digging
and hard vaulting
to build the tunnel.*

Eric, Michael and Oliver crawled through the tunnel one cold October day and made it outside the prison fence. They eventually traveled all the way through Germany and arrived back in England to tell their story of the amazing vaulting horse of Stalag Luft III.

Escape from the Tower of London

Even after George I, a Protestant, became King of England in 1714, the fifth Earl of Nithsdale continued to support the Catholic Stuart cause. But he was charged with treason and sent to the Tower of London for execution.

Lady Nithsdale became friends with her husband's guards, even giving them tips on each visit. On Friday, February 23, 1716, the day before the scheduled execution, she took her maid and two friends, Mrs. Betty Mills and Miss Catherine Hilton, for a "last visit." Mrs. Mills, a large woman, wore a cape big enough to fit over Lord Nithsdale. Miss Hilton, a thin woman, wore two capes.

At first, only Lady Nithsdale and Miss Hilton went to the cell, leaving the other two ladies on the stairway. Miss Hilton left one of her capes in the cell and then sent up the maid. Part of the plan was to confuse the guards by a constant coming and going.

Mrs. Mills went up next and exchanged her large cape for the one left behind by Miss Hilton. Lady Nithsdale quickly dressed her husband in this cape and covered his black beard with a handkerchief. As she led him from the cell, she pretended that she was consoling a sobbing "Betty." At the bottom of the stairs, the maid led Nithsdale away, and his wife returned to the cell, pretending to visit him one more "last time." She then shut the door on the empty cell and asked the guards to please give her husband a few moments of agonized peace. They agreed and were thus completely outsmarted!

Lord Nithsdale hid in a friend's home for two days. Then, disguised as a diplomat, he escaped to Rome where he and his brave wife lived the rest of their lives in peace.

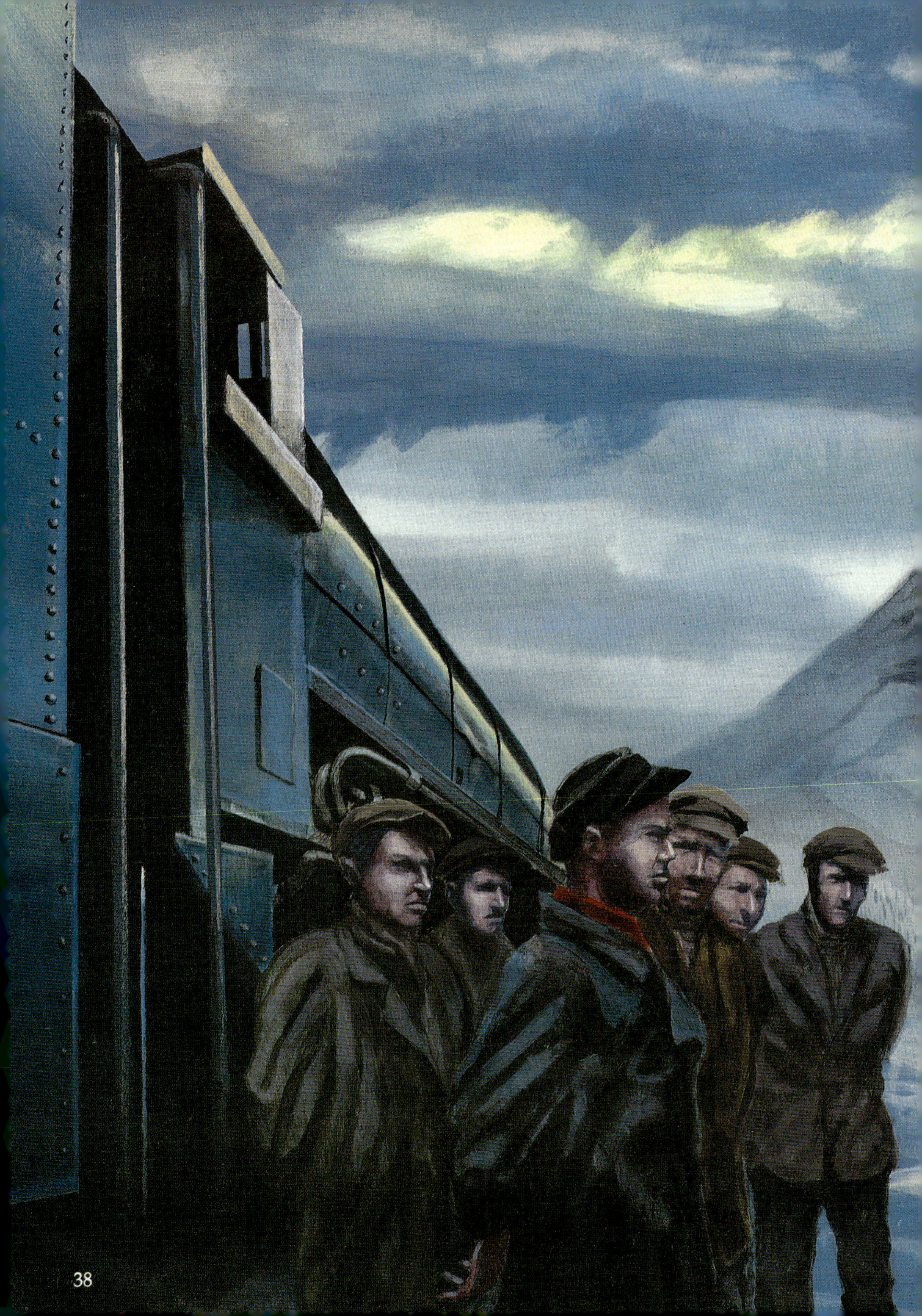

JOURNEY TO FREEDOM

In the fall of 1939, Polish Army lieutenant Slavomir Rawicz was arrested by the Soviet Secret Police and charged with spying. Held in the notorious Kharkov Prison in Moscow for nearly a year, he was subjected to torture at the hands of his captors. Throughout his detention, however, Slavomir continued to claim he was innocent. Nevertheless, at trial he was pronounced guilty of spying and sentenced to twenty-five years forced labor in Siberia.

The journey to Camp No. 303, south of the Arctic Circle, was long and tiring. The prisoners were herded into unheated cattle cars for the long trip by rail. Then they had to walk on foot through the bitter cold Siberian winter for the final fifteen hundred kilometers (one thousand miles).

*Soon after his arrival
in the camp, Slavomir Rawicz
began to plan his escape.*

Initially Rawicz was assigned to work with the forest labor force. One month after his arrival at the camp, he volunteered for a job making skis. With this move, his bread ration increased. This enabled Rawicz to hoard provisions to have if he were successful with his escape.

Several weeks later a request was made by the commandant for someone to repair his radio. Again Rawicz volunteered his services. Over the next four weeks he made numerous visits to the commandant's house to work on the radio. During this time he was befriended by the man's wife. Through her, he obtained clothing and food. He added this to what he and his six carefully selected companions had been able to gather and conceal in preparation for their journey to freedom.

It was agreed in advance that the route offering the greatest chance for success was south to Afghanistan or India. But both of these routes were long and covered treacherous terrain. They had planned to escape during a snow storm since the densely falling snow would quickly cover their tracks and make it harder for the search party to find them.

One night in April, the weather conditions were perfectly suited for their escape. The seven prisoners crept soundlessly out of their barracks. One after the other they wriggled under the barbed wire fence around Camp No. 303, crossed over the steep-sided dry moat, scaled the high wooden fence, eluded guards and guard dogs in the patrol area, and finally climbed over the final stockade. With the camp at their backs, they ran south through the deep forest the rest of that night and half the next day, hardly stopping to catch their breath in the freezing air.

Exhausted, unable to go any farther, they built a shelter near a huge tree and crowded together in their crude house of snow and branches. Each man permitted himself only a small piece of bread for his meal that night. They did not have much food and knew it could be a long time before finding more.

The escapees slept through the rest of that day, each man taking his turn on guard until a few hours after nightfall when they started traveling again. They continued to rest during the day and travel by night for the next few days. They finally felt safe enough to travel by day when no signs of their searchers were seen.

It wasn't until the eighth or ninth night that they allowed themselves the luxury of a fire and were able to enjoy their first hot dinner.

The next day the group of seven fugitives walked across the ice covered Lena River. They continued traveling as far as they could during the day and at night they rested and tried to keep warm.

Some days later the group found a full-grown male deer, its antlers entwined in the tangled roots of an uprooted tree. Putting the poor animal out of its misery, they killed it. Unable to carry such a large amount of meat, they ate what they could and carried some in their packs. They prepared the skin and made it into fourteen pairs of moccasins.

They reached Lake Baikal toward the end of May. Near the lake they found a seventeen-year-old Ukrainian girl named Kristina, also a fugitive from a labor camp. She joined them on their trek and became like a sister to the seven men.

It was six weeks since the prisoners had made their escape and summer was upon them. During the warm daylight hours they needed only light clothing, but at night they donned their fur vests to protect themselves from the chilly air.

They had been without food for several days when they met up with an old woodcutter who shared a small amount of bread, pork and fish with them. Knowing it might be days before finding more food, the group of tired travelers only ate small amounts at one time. Soon the fugitives were near the border of Outer Mongolia. Daylight travel was becoming more hazardous since the area had many more people. They had to return to nighttime marches.

Finally, their hunger was so great they had to raid a village and steal a small pig. They cooked it and ate as much as they could, glad for the chance to fill their packs with enough food for several days.

They crossed the Russo-Mongolian border in the second week of June and were filled with a great feeling of relief. At last, they were out of Siberia. In just over sixty days they had traveled close to two thousand kilometers (twelve hundred miles). Their destination - India - was almost twice that distance.

For the next eight days their route took them over a mountain range. Then the coolness of the mountains gave way to the oppressive heat of a plain, and traveling became much more difficult.

In August, they entered the Gobi Desert with little food and no water. They sucked on pebbles to create saliva, and in the hottest part of the day they made shelters by draping jackets over sticks dug into the sand.

On the seventh day an oasis appeared ahead of them. The travelers thought they were dreaming. They forced themselves to trudge on until they reached the water. They crouched down and drank the water like animals.

The weary group discovered some fresh bones with pieces of meat still attached. They divided these and ate with great eagerness. A caravan must have recently passed by and left the bones and pieces of wire. After eating and drinking, the travelers gathered the wire and continued their journey. For the next three weeks, their only food was snake meat.

They finally reached the end of the desert and entered Tibet. Here the land was very rugged with mountainous terrain. They met an old shepherd who fed them well and sent them on their way with a sheepskin which they later made into six pairs of warm mitts.

Over the next three months they walked almost twenty-five hundred kilometers (about fifteen hundred miles) over rough and rugged terrain. The Tibetan villagers were very kind to the travelers and, with their offers of food and lodging, the fugitives were able to continue the journey.

By November, they were in barren land again and were forced to go hungry for days at a time. The hills increased in size and climbing became more difficult. They used the wire they had found at the oasis by tying the pieces together to make a climbing rope. Their journey through the Himalayas lasted until the end of March. They traveled over massive peaks in freezing temperatures and thin air.

Not all of them made it. Cold, heat, lack of food and the rugged terrain proved to be too much for some of them. The four men who survived were exhausted, filthy and hungry as they finally entered India and freedom. In the distance they saw a small band of men marching in their direction. The weary survivors were too weak to cry out but as the soldiers drew near, the men danced around wildly with relief before each one collapsed on the ground.

The journey had lasted twelve long months and had taken them over sixty-five hundred kilometers (four thousand miles) of punishing terrain. At last they were free and safe. They all spent time recuperating in a Calcutta hospital. They were truly amazed that they had survived such a daring escape.

Escape of a 'Sewer Rat'

On October 27, 1976, seven men from various parts of France were arrested by the French police. They confessed that they had been involved in "the heist of the century" - the incredible robbery of the Societè Generale bank in Nice. The mastermind behind the heist, Albert Spaggiare, was also captured. Now, several months after the robbery, Albert waited in handcuffs outside a courtroom in Nice, France. He had been ordered to tell the judge all details of the robbery.

Albert began his story. He thought back to the beginning - when he first decided to rob the bank. It was 1974, and Albert had arrived at the bank wanting to rent a safety deposit box in the vault. That very day the idea to rob the bank began to grow inside his mind. Albert returned to the bank and took photographs of the inside of the vault. Then he went to town council and, pretending he was a builder, obtained the blueprints for the underground area surrounding the bank. Albert's plan: To travel through the sewers and then dig an underground tunnel up to the bank wall where the vault stood.

Over the next four months, Albert went to court and told the judge how he and his men, the other 'sewer rats' as they were called, went about robbing the bank.

They had entered the sewers through a manhole in an underground parking lot not far from the bank. They traveled as close to the bank as they could in the sewers and then began to tunnel toward the bank through the wall. The work was difficult and very tiring. The men had to reinforce the walls of their tunnel with cement and wooden beams. They couldn't take the risk of having the tunnel cave in on them while they were working. Albert told the judge how tired and discouraged the men became as the weeks of tunneling turned into two months. They were almost at their limits when - clunk! - they hit the heavy cement wall of the bank.

Their tiredness forgotten, the men took turns drilling and chipping the cement. The wall of the bank was so thick that it took the men over fourteen hours to break through. It was Saturday, July 17, and they didn't have much time left. They had to be far away from the bank when it opened on the following Monday morning.

The hole through the wall wasn't big enough for the men to get through. Another five hours were needed to widen the hole. Finally, early Sunday morning, Albert wiggled through the hole. He could hardly believe it when he stood up inside the vault. Several other men crawled through the hole and worked at sealing the door to the vault by welding it at the seams. This would give them extra time to get away since bank officials wouldn't be able to easily open the vault door on Monday morning.

With this completed, the men turned on the lights inside the vault. They looked around in wonder - four thousand safety deposit boxes plus gold and cash, were all within their reach. The men began to laugh hysterically. They couldn't believe that they'd actually succeeded. All their work over the past two months had been well worth it.

They celebrated with a meal of fruit, sausage, pizza and wine. After this short rest, the men worked in pairs opening the safety deposit boxes and safes with cash and gold in them. They only took cash, gold and precious stones - nothing was removed that could be traced.

The 'sewer rats' worked as fast as they could. Suddenly, their time was up - it was 5:00 a.m. Monday morning, and Albert told his men it was time to pack up and get out. They left pieces of equipment everywhere. Albert believed that this would stall the police for awhile. They would have to gather the equipment, articles of clothing, scattered checks, garbage and discarded jewelry to examine it for markings and fingerprints.

Before Albert left the bank, he wrote a message on the wall of the vault to the police and bank officials. It read, "Sans armes, sans haine, et sans violence" - No guns, no hatred, no violence. With that, Albert joined his men in the sewers and had the stolen goods taken in wheelbarrel loads to waiting vehicles. They were still nervous and weren't out of danger yet. Finally they drove out of the town center victorious! They had successfully robbed the Societè Generale of millions and millions of dollars. And they had all gotten away without being caught by the police.

But all that was months ago! After following hundreds of clues left behind by the carelessness of the 'sewer rats,' the police had caught up with them. That was how Albert found himself in front of a judge telling his story. It seemed as if Albert was doomed to spending several years in jail for robbery. At least that's what most people thought.

But most people didn't know Albert. He had an adventurous spirit, and his piercing mind was always whirling. As he spoke to the judge in March of 1977, he walked close to the window in the courtroom. His handcuffs had been removed earlier, and his hands were free. Suddenly, Albert jumped out of the window. The people in the courtroom gasped! They thought that Albert had jumped to his death. Instead, Albert had landed on a ledge, jumped down from the ledge onto a car roof and rolled onto the road. There a motorcycle was waiting with a driver. Albert jumped on the back and with a grin on his face, he shouted, "Au revoir."

After Albert's escape from the courthouse, the police searched for him everywhere. Albert was nowhere to be found. He had simply vanished. Months later, the Nice police received a post card from Albert. It had been mailed locally, but the police never found a sign of Albert - the man who had masterminded the most spectacular bank robbery in history and then escaped!

44

ESCAPE TO THE PAST

George Stewart squeezed his eyes shut and then opened them quickly again. No, he wasn't dreaming - there in front of him was a De Havilland Mosquito fighter-bomber and he was going to fly it, just as he had done almost forty-five years ago.

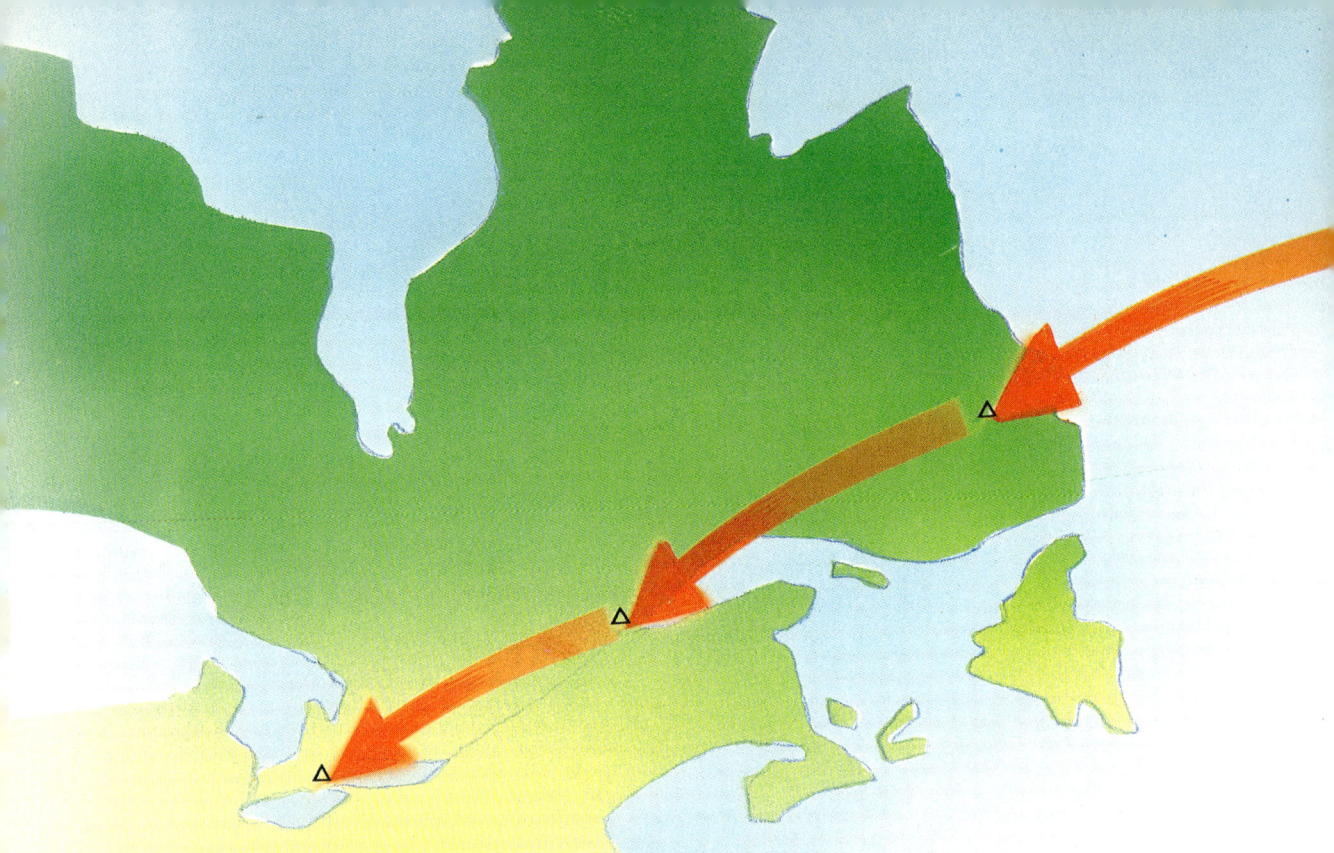

Not exactly "just as he had done" then, because in 1943 the Second World War was at its height, a terrifying time as the British, the Americans, the Canadians, the Russians, and their allies fought against the German Nazis and their Italian and Japanese partners. George thought back to that terrifying time when he was only nineteen but already an experienced Mosquito pilot in the skies over Europe.

Now in October of 1987, George was about to escape to his past. He and another pilot were actually going to fly a Mosquito from England to North America, over the Atlantic to a new home in Florida. So this would be a different kind of trip from those George used to make during the war. No one would be shooting at him as he and his fellow pilot flew from England to Scotland, Iceland, Greenland and Canada.

Yet, as he stood there before the lovely Mosquito, George thought of those long-ago nights on "Intruder" operations when he and others of his squadron would fly near enemy night-fighter airfields and, using cannons and bombs, harass the German aircraft as they attempted to land and take off. He remembered how on moonlit nights, after doing airfield patrols, he would shoot up "enemy supply trains" or perhaps do a "spoof" operation high over Cologne or other German cities nearby. A "spoof" was an attempt, often highly successful, to deceive the enemy into believing that the "spoof" aircraft were the main bombing force on that particular night and hence cause them to send their night fighters away from the bombers toward the Mosquitos - which, being so very fast, would easily escape. And then there were the daylight escort operations when they flew with the big Lancasters, those big four-engined bombers that, without the Mosquitos for protection, would normally fly only at night.

After George finished two tours of operations and had been awarded the Distinguished Flying Cross, he returned to Canada to instruct other pilots on Mosquitos. He even went to China, in 1947, to show that country's pilots how to fly his favorite airplane. When he returned he flew P51 Mustangs with 424 (City of Hamilton) Reserve Squadron. Then for a long time, over ten years, he did no flying at all, but with the founding of the Canadian Warplane Heritage at Mount Hope, near Hamilton, George was able to fulfil the dream of most ex-wartime pilots - fly those marvellous airplanes of the past, everything from the Tiger Moth to the Spitfire! George has flown them all again. But until now, not the Mosquito.

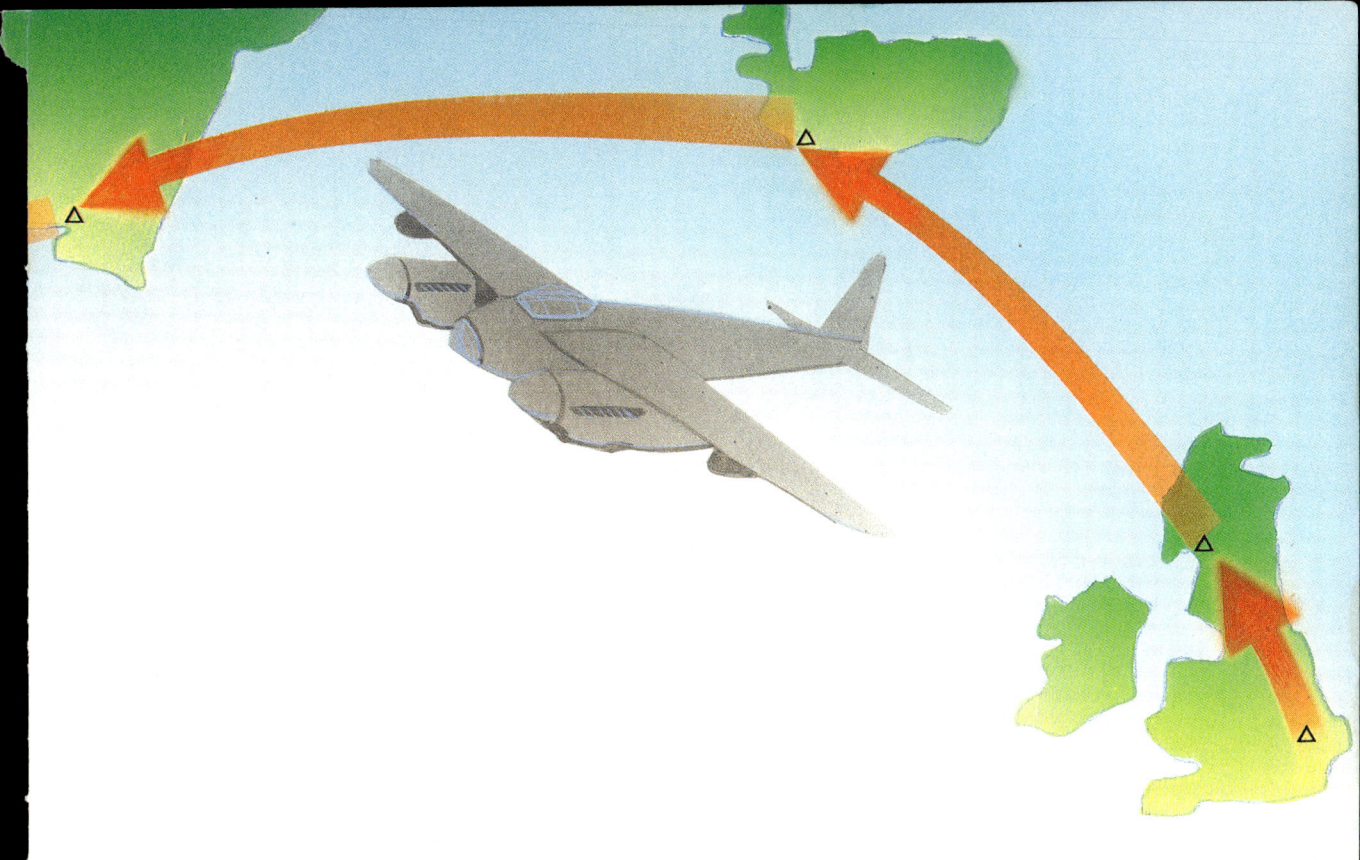

It was because of his varied experience that George was asked to co-pilot the Mosquito, bought by Mr. Kermit Weeks of Florida, across the Atlantic. Mr. Weeks had bought the aircraft for £100,000 on his twenty-eighth birthday in 1981, but it required another £100,000 and six years to restore it to its original condition. There is only one other Mosquito in the world still flying, owned by British Aerospace, and Mr. Weeks wanted his plane to be brought to his museum in Florida, where it could fly, with his other vintage aircraft, in airshows and demonstrations. Mr. George Aird, a former test pilot for British Aerospace, had agreed to captain the flight across and George, with his extensive experience in flying World War II aircraft and particularly the Mosquito, was asked to be the other man in the cockpit with Captain Aird.

And now the time to leave had arrived! George and his fellow-pilot climbed up the short ladder into the small cockpit area that, off and on, would be their home for the next five days. They were dressed warmly and had oxygen masks close by. Their flight would take them to high altitudes and cold, thin air; even icing of the wing surfaces could be a serious problem, almost as serious as an enemy shooting at them!

The Mosquito taxied along the perimeter at RAF Station Benson, the same base that is home to the aircraft of the Queen's Flight. The tower gave them takeoff clearance, the machine, laden with fuel, picked up speed - the wheels came off the ground and they were airborne! George was almost speechless with delight as he felt the thrust of the powerful Merlin engines and heard their so-distinctive sound. The large town below their right wing became rapidly smaller as the Mosquito climbed skyward at almost two hundred mph and headed toward Prestwick, Scotland, their first refuelling stop. Suddenly, as though out of the blue, appeared the British Aerospace Mosquito, the only other in the whole world! A fast "civilian" aircraft flew alongside and took pictures of the historic moment, probably the last time ever that two Mosquitos would fly in formation.

After staying overnight in Prestwick, George and his captain took off for Iceland and, after just over four hours, landed at Reykjavik. Soon they were airborne for Greenland and climbing above cloud to ten thousand feet, but as they approached the great whiteness of Greenland, they were forced to don their oxygen masks and climb to fourteen thousand feet to get safely above that country's great ice caps. As the evening sky darkened behind them, they landed at Narsarsuaq Airport, refuelled the "Mossie" and "turned in" for a much-needed night's rest.

The next morning, off to Goose Bay, Labrador, but again the weather was deteriorating and upon reaching Goose Bay, George and Captain Aird decided to shelter their precious plane in the RAF hangar there and carry on the following morning. But they awoke to a relentless, driving rain and not until late in the afternoon could they take off for Ottawa, their second-to-last stop.

But again darkness began to catch up with them and so they decided to head for Quebec City and then fly non-stop to Hamilton the next day. It had been many years since George and Captain Aird had flown a Mosquito at night and they did not wish to risk the airplane or their lives merely for the sake of a few hours. And it had started to rain again.

The next day dawned in a light drizzle, not enough to deter the "Mossie" and its crew. Within three hours they were over Mount Hope airport. Down below was a great crowd of enthusiastic well-wishers (it was Saturday) and in appreciation of such a welcome, the beautiful airplane flew three thrilling low, fast passes just above the main runway.

George undid his safety belt and climbed down the ladder. The dream was over but it was a dream come true. What incredible luck! He had done what has been described as impossible - he had actually repeated the past! He had escaped from the everyday life that most of us have to live and had relived moments of his life of nearly forty-five years before.

As Captain Aird taxied away for the final, relatively safe, leg of the Mosquito's flight to Florida, George Stewart would have been willing to swear that 1943 was still there and he was nineteen again.